Mommy Daddy Evan Sage

Mommy Daddy Evan Sage

POEMS BY
Eric McHenry

ILLUSTRATIONS BY
Nicholas Garland

First published in 2011 by

THE WAYWISER PRESS

Bench House, 82 London Road, Chipping Norton, Oxon OX7 5FN, UK
P.O. Box 6205, Baltimore, MD 21206, USA
http://waywiser-press.com

Editor-in-Chief
Philip Hoy

Senior American Editor
Joseph Harrison

Associate Editors
Eric McHenry   Clive Watkins   Greg Williamson

ISBN 978-1-904130-45-1

Printed and bound by
T.J. International Ltd., Padstow, Cornwall, PL28 8RW

for Sonja, Evan and Sage, of course, and for Duncan Brown

&

for Milo and Eva

"Evan, don't fill up on bread.
Eat your broccoli," I said.
He pointed to the florets: "These
aren't broccoli," he said. "They're trees.
And they provide a shady spot
for this hot dog, who's very hot."
"I see," I said. "In that case, please
eat your dog and then your trees."

"Don't bite your knee," I said to Sage.
"You're almost two. Please act your age."
"I won't be two for two more months,"
she said, "and I'll be one just once!
If I don't bite my knee right now,
when will I?" Then she bit it. "Ow!
My knee!" she said, and rubbed her knee.
I shook my head. "Don't look at me."

Sage pretty much knows
where everything goes.
She's got enough info to go on:
dresses in dressers,
books in the bookcase,
toys in the toilet, and so on.

"Eat your trees," I said to Evan.
"There's one, two, three, four, five, six, seven
trees on your plate, and you should eat 'em.
This table's not an arboretum."
Then Evan pointed to the eight
uneaten trees on my own plate:
"Daddy, eat your broccoli,
and don't eat it so talk-ily."

"No school today," I whispered. "Snow."
Evan sat up and stretched. "I know."
"You know?" I said, crestfallen. "How?"
"You told me so," he said. "Just now."

"I think there ought to be a guy,"
said Evan, "with one X-ray eye,
and extra fingers, who can swallow
top-secret files because he's hollow,
except that he contains a motor
that turns a helicopter rotor
that's where his shoulder blade should be,
and who speaks Dolphin, and who's me."

"Stand still as fast as you can,"
Sage said. So I did, and she ran
out of the room and back in.
Then she said, "I win."

In the yard, in the dust-colored snow,
little legs were beginning to show.
Evan sighed, "What a beautiful thing:
It's the first action figure of spring."

"I'M EV-1," Evan monotoned.
"I'M ROBOT-BRAINED AND ROBOT-BONED.
UNLIKE YOUR INEFFICIENT DAUGHTER,
I DON'T REQUIRE THIS FOOD AND WATER."
He rose to leave, but Mommy caught him.
"Sit down," she said, "on your robottom."

"Evan is seven. You are two,"
I said. "Why would I let you do
the things a seven-year-old does?"
Sage rubbed her brow and sighed. "Be*cause*
of what you said yourself. It's true:
Evan is seven. I am too."

"You think I'm going to stop at knees?
I can bite anything I please!"
"All right," I told Sage. "Bite your nose."
"All right," she said. "I will. Here goes."

"Are caterpillars always slow?"
Sage asked her brother. "Yes, and no,
depending on your point of view,"
he told her. "What looks slow to you
may look more like a lightning bolt
shot from a caterpillarpult
to something that can barely budge,
like grass or moss or cold hot fudge.
And let's be honest: We don't know
how fast this little guy can go
when motivated. Maybe he'd
turn on his secret hyperspeed
if he were really scared, or late,
or traveling on the interstate.
Maybe he takes it slow and steady
because he's always there already."

Our newest house pet, Lightning Buggy,
shares a terrarium with Sluggy,
Katydiddy, Anty, Ticky,
Bumblebee-y, Walking Sticky,
Monarchy the Butterfly,
a bug we can't identify
that looks just like a grape, but furry,
and a cicada named Ron Murray.

"Rats!" said Sage, whose magic marker
refused to color any darker.
"Uh-oh. I think I hear them comin',"
I said. "Be careful what you summon.
Rats are responsive. If you call
too loudly you might get them all.
Are you prepared to deal with that?"
She scratched her head. "I guess not. Rat."

"It might work with a panther," Evan said,
"but if you see a vulture, don't play dead."

"A monkey and an ape are not the same," said Sage. "The monkey has a longer name."

"No, I'm not saying Sage is really a spy," said Evan. "That's just silly. I'm simply asking you to keep an eye on her when I'm asleep, ask lots of questions, and consider making her wear this small transmitter."

"The N is missing from the end
of my first name! I've been de-N'd!"
said Eva. "And don't call me that!
Eva's a girl's name," he spat.
"Calm down. You'll get it back again.
Nobody steals the letter N,"
I said. He stomped off in a rage.
"What's he so mad about?" said Snage.

"Evan, what's the magic word?"
I asked. I guess he hadn't heard
that it was "Please," because he said
"Alakazam-kazoo" instead,
which I suspect (I can't be certain)
is why I'm now a shower curtain.

Sage-y had a little lamb.
She named it Alligator.
That made Aunt Lucy laugh and laugh.
Then Alligator ate her.

"You won't see Mommy in a hurry,"
said Evan. "You'll see something blurry."

"I'll be the girl who tries to catch you," said Sage, "and you can be the statue."

"A consequence," Sage said, "is when you take my favorite toy away and I look at the floor and say 'Sorry' and get it back again."

"I love your name. I think it's great,"
I said. "And yet I hesitate
to put it on our license plate.
Why can't you wait until you're grown?
Then you can put it on your own."
"By then," said Evan, "I'll be known
as 'Special Agent Roger Strong,
the Ace of Hearts,' and that's too long."

"Which of these names do you prefer –
Jehoshaphat or Cocklebur?"
said Evan. "For yourself, I mean."
"That isn't much to choose between,"
I said. "I think I'll keep my name."
"No, pick!" he said. "It's just a game."
"Okay, I'll take Jehoshaphat."
"Why would you want a name like that?"

"That N was nothing. R's the letter
Sage really, really wants to get her
hands on," I said. "And we can't let her."

Evan looked up. His eyes were large.
"You're right! She'll act like she's in charge
of *everybody* when she's Sarge."

"To brush your teeth or pee or get a drink:
Each one of those excuses is, I think,
legitimate, unlike the one you gave.
Go back to bed, Sage. You don't need to shave."

"What if you see a fiery ball
the size of a Toyota fall
into your favorite flower bed?"
"I don't know, Evan," Mommy said.
I'll probably be terrified."
"You won't be when the flames subside
and I step out of it and say,
'I'm going to park this here, okay?'"

On Halloween, Sage always eats a
gigantic slice of garlic pizza,
and if you ask her why she'll say,
"It keeps the Draculas away,"
which, frankly, I suspect is true.
It works on other people too.

"Do you still love me when you're mad?"
"Of course!" I told Sage. "I'm your dad.
So when you fuss or make a mess,
it doesn't make me love you less."
She said that made her feel much better,
and wiped her nose on my new sweater.

A Note About Eric McHenry

Eric McHenry grew up in Topeka, Kansas and earned degrees from Beloit College and Boston University. His first book of poems, *Potscrubber Lullabies* (Waywiser, 2006), won the Kate Tufts Discovery Award, and in 2010 *Poetry Northwest* awarded him the Theodore Roethke Prize. He is a contributing editor of *Columbia* magazine and has written about poetry for the *New York Times Book Review*, *Parnassus: Poetry in Review*, the *San Francisco Chronicle*, the *Boston Globe* and *Slate*. He lives in Topeka with his wife, Sonja, and their two children, Evan and Sage, and teaches creative writing at Washburn University.

A Note About Nicholas Garland

Nicholas Garland was born in London in 1935 and from 1947 lived in New Zealand. He returned to London to study at the Slade School of Fine Art. Later he worked as a Stage Manager at the Royal Court Theatre and directed shows at Peter Cook's Establishment Club. With Barry Humphries he created the Barry McKenzie strip for *Private Eye* and quit the theatre to become a political cartoonist. He has also illustrated a number of books, by John Fuller, Wendy Cope, James Fenton and Alex Garland among others. He is married and has four children and six grandchildren.

Other books from Waywiser

Other books from Waywiser

Mark Strand, *Blizzard of One*
Bradford Gray Telford, *Perfect Hurt*
Cody Walker, *Shuffle and Breakdown*
Deborah Warren, *The Size of Happiness*
Clive Watkins, *Jigsaw*
Richard Wilbur, *Anterooms*
Richard Wilbur, *Mayflies*
Richard Wilbur, *Collected Poems 1943-2004*
Norman Williams, *One Unblinking Eye*
Greg Williamson, *A Most Marvelous Piece of Luck*

FICTION

Gregory Heath, *The Entire Animal*
Matthew Yorke, *Chancing It*

ILLUSTRATED

Nicholas Garland, *I wish ...*

NON-FICTION

Neil Berry, *Articles of Faith:*
The Story of British Intellectual Journalism
Mark Ford, *A Driftwood Altar: Essays and Reviews*
Richard Wollheim, *Germs: A Memoir of Childhood*